HOPE TO COPE:
The Loss of a Child

LaVinia Young

Kingdom Builders Publications LLC

© 2022 LaVinia B. Young
Hope to Cope: The Loss of a Child
Kingdom Builders Publications, LLC

Paperback
ISBN: 978-0-578-33476-9
LCCN: 2022900800

Hardback
ISBN: 2370001601987
LCCN: 2021925916

Author
LaVinia Young

Editor
Lakisha S. Forrester

Publisher
Kingdom Builders Publications, LLC

Cover Design
LoMar Designs
Photo 128633664 © Tommaso79 | Dreamstime.com

Printed in the USA

All rights reserved. No part of this book may be reproduced or transmitted in any form or by any means without written permission from the author.

Scripture quotations marked ESV are taken from The Holy Bible, English Standard Version.

Scriptures marked KJV are taken from the King James Version.

Scriptures marked NIV are taken from The Holy Bible, New International Version.

Scriptures marked NKJV are taken from the New King James Version.

Scriptures marked RSV are taken from the Revised Standard Version.

Dedication

This book is dedicated to the Spirit of the Living God. Father, thank you for strengthening me to author this piece. I could not have accomplished this without your help.

You blessed me with three children, all of whom have made me proud. Dwayne, Dawn, and Shannon, I love you dearly. Children, your father was an amazing man. Even though he is not here in the physical, he is still so very much alive living through you, his seed, his offspring.

To parents who are surviving child loss, God is your strength and comforter. He will repair your shattered and broken hearts. My prayer is that this book will be of help on your journey to healing and restoration.

Acknowledgments

During our time of bereavement, there were so many people who came alongside us to help lift the burden. To everyone who contributed in any way (phone calls, sympathy cards, and visitations), I acknowledge and thank you.

The Young family, you traveled afar to support and lift our arms. That is what family does. I appreciate each and every one of you.

My nieces, nephews, cousins, and friends who traveled to be with us, you are all uniquely special to my heart. I will not forget your labors of love.

Pastor Tommy and Lady Faye Jackson and my True Word Church of Evangelical Christian Church Ministries (E.C.C.M.) family, thank you for everything you contributed, especially your prayers.

Bishop (Dr.) Mikel and Lady Debra Brown and the Joy Center family, thank you for your prayers and monetary gifts.

Bishop Dublin and Elect Lady Elaine Johnson of Bible Way Pentecostal Church of Savannah, Georgia, thank you for traveling to support us with your gifts of love.

Apostle Steven and Pastor Dee Spencer and the El Shaddai Ministry family, you all went over and above with supplies and love.

Pastor Kevin and Evangelist Tina Washington, Missionary Marie, and Thomas Green, thank you.

To a special young lady that is dear to my heart, Marlynda Lawhorn, I acknowledge you for the love and support you've given to us.

I love you all!

Contents

Dedication v

Acknowledgments vi

Contents viii

Prologue ix

Introduction x

Shannon's Foundation 11

Shannon's Big Heart 21

Why So Soon? 30

Am I in Denial? 36

Shattered, Not Broken 39

Insensitivity of the Heart 44

Accepting the Loss 52

Strong Support System 61

A Prayer for You 67

Epilogue 69

Tribute 70

About the Author 94

Prologue

Shannon.

Oh how I love the sound of that name.

Recently, I did an internet search to find out what my son's name means. It is of Irish origin and it means "Old River"[1] and "Wise River,"[2] which makes me think of a river that flows and gives life. In fact, Ireland's longest river is the River Shannon.[3]

Also in Irish, Shannon's name means "Possessor of Wisdom."[4]

In Hebrew, his name means "God is gracious."[5]

We know that naming a child is something that is of utmost importance because it has a lasting impact. To find out that those were the phrases I spoke over him each and every time I called his name makes my heart glad.

---

[1] https://kidal.com/baby-names/meaning-of/shannon
[2] https://www.kidpaw.com/names/shannon
[3] https://discovertheshannon.com/river-shannon-histor/
[4] https://www.kidpaw.com/names/shannon
[5] https://www.thenamemeaning.com/shannon/

Introduction

On February 25, 2021, I experienced severe trauma when my son, Shannon – young, vibrant, and full of life at 41 years old – was tragically taken from us.

In my grief, I learned that the hurt is still the same, whether the child was an infant or fifty plus years, or if they died naturally or tragically, because a part of you has been taken away.

During this time in my life, I relied heavily on my Lord and Savior, Jesus Christ. He is our example in dealing with grief. He is a High Priest who knows what it is to experience loss and is able to sympathize "with the feeling of our infirmities" (**Hebrews 4:15**, KJV). His grief and concern for us led Him to willingly submit to the sacrificial pangs of physical death on the Cross. We were worth it to Jesus then, and we are worth it to Him now.

So whatever trauma you may be experiencing or have experienced, I pray you know that

He is the answer. May this book be a blessing to you, a tool to help heal your broken, shattered heart, and as a result of you being blessed, you will pass it on to help others who have been traumatized by the loss of a loved one, so they too can experience the healing power of God.

Shannon's Foundation

After giving birth to our son, Dwayne and daughter, Dawn, my husband and I decided it was time to stop having children. We made a doctor's appointment to discuss the tubal ligation procedure to have my tubes tied. After the examination, the doctor smiled and said, "I cannot do the procedure because you are pregnant."

My husband was in the waiting room. He heard my outburst of loud laughter and began to wonder if everything was alright with me. I believe I was in shock. After all, just a few months prior I had given birth to Dawn.

During childbirth, the doctor almost dropped Shannon on his head but caught him. When my son got older, I told him about the story. He said he wished he could find that doctor to thank him.

When Shannon was in his toddler and adolescent years, I called him mischievous because of his behavior. His playful attitude would sometimes cause troubles. He would throw rocks, hide his hands, and say, "I didn't do it. Dawn did it!" Because of their close births, Dawn and Shannon were considered Irish twins. That's when a mother has two children 12 to 18 months apart.

When I was pregnant with Shannon, I learned the importance of reading and speaking to your baby in the womb. (I didn't have that knowledge during my first two pregnancies.) Because of that small act, Shannon came out loving to read. He started reading between the ages of three and four, so I decided not to spend money on an academic Head Start program and homeschool him myself. We had the best time together with him learning and me teaching. He thrived exponentially because I involved him in practical, hands-on activities. I taught him the alphabets, numbers, shapes, patterns, and how to sound out words.

Shannon developed a habit of reading. After reading *Little Toot*[6] and reciting, "I think I

---

[6] Hardie Gramatky, 1939

can, I think I can" from *The Little Engine That Could*,[7] my son knew without a doubt there was nothing in this world he could not accomplish.

Shannon was a sharp little boy. He was smart, strong, and determined to win. He had what older adults would call "an old man's brain." He loved hanging out with my father, the Late Solomon Young and his Godfather, the late Ulysses Washington and gleaning from their wisdom.

The third book my son read was by Maurice Sendak. It was about a little boy named Pierre who didn't care about anything until he met a lion, and not caring became a problem.[8] As Shannon grew, this book became his reality because he developed an "I don't care attitude." The lesson he learned at an early age that "I don't care" was not an appropriate answer must have slipped his mind.

---

[7] Watty Piper, 1930
[8] Pierre: A Cautionary Tale in Five Chapters and a Prologue, 1962

Because I taught him at home, he was bored by the classroom setting when he entered public school at age six. He didn't have any problems in the first grade, probably because he went to school medicated on Benadryl for allergies. His attention span became a problem when he was in the second and third grade. I received numerous phone calls from his school to discuss his destructive attitude. Shannon already knew how to read and count to 100, so he felt that he was ahead of his class, and he was. I believe this led to him being uninterested and acting out.

He talked back to his teachers and refused to complete class assignments. He spent a lot of time daydreaming, talking, and disrupting the classroom. School was a playground for him. Smart, yes, but he did not like doing homework assignments either. He would come home with no book bag and say it was in his locker because he didn't have any homework.

His teenage years was where the rubber met the road – tumultuous, fierce, hectic, and stormy. I always gave my children space to express what they were feeling or dealing with. But there was always a line drawn in the sand. If they crossed that line, there would be consequences that followed. They knew how far to go.

When you hear a parent say, "I'm having teenage problems." Those words were an understatement for me at that time. I would have loved to have their kind of problems considering all our family was facing.

We all have that child or children that keeps us on our knees. Shannon was that child. I wanted to free him from his sinful activities, but he had a mind of his own, and no one, not even his parents could instruct him. His strong will guided him more than anything or anyone trying to help him.

It is only fair to give him credit for teaching me how to war in the spirit for our family. He taught me spiritual warfare because I stayed before God on his behalf. I learned that it is always best to pray about everything and give it to the Lord, even if it's your own children.

Shannon used to say, "Mommy, I do what all boys at my age do, but I will do nothing to hurt you." My son was a handful, but he never bold-faced disrespected me. As a concerned parent, when my parenting skills didn't seem to work, I got the authorities involved to scare him into doing right before he ends up committing a crime. I tried to get him arrested without having committed any illegal crime. The authorities said they couldn't carry out my request, but they did recommend family counseling. *No, thank you! Talking was not working!*

Back then, they did not have programs like Scared Straight, prison tours, and weekend lock downs like they do today. So the phrase "my hands are full" resulted in me checking different avenues that might be able to help me show him the importance of obeying school and home rules.

In-school and out-of-school suspension for fighting and disobeying security officers became his norm. He did not like school. I sat in many principals' offices where we tried to instruct him on the importance of his education. Because of his disciplinary problems, we transferred him from school to school, thinking that a new environment would change his attitude.

We eventually enrolled him into an alternative school, at his high school principal's request. Shannon stayed on campus Monday through Friday, came home on the weekend, and returned to school on Sunday. The staff was surprised that he enrolled without an order from the authorities because the majority, if not all the students, were there by court order.

He did great there for a while and was on the honor roll until he got tired of being bullied. He was always in fights with other boys who tried to gang up on him on different occasions. He decided to take it upon himself and take matters in his own hands. Unbeknownst to me, he got a gun from a friend and took it to school for protection. One day while walking down the hall, the gun fell from his pocket. Someone saw it and reported it to the principal. Shannon was arrested, charged with possessing a handgun under the age of 18, unlawful possession of a stolen gun, and having a dangerous weapon on federal property. When he had to go to court for the gun charge, he said he did not want me in the courtroom and that he could handle it by himself…and he did, with a few phone calls. He was released on a Personal Recognizance or PR bond. His bond was waved and he was put on parole. He went through the necessary steps and completed his parole without a problem. He never returned to that school, and he was expelled for the remainder of the school year. He picked up other trades and did well for himself.

At home, he was also a handful. He would sneak girls into his bedroom that was next to the garage, which was easy access of course. My bedroom was on the other end of the house. The Holy Spirit would gently say, "Check Shannon's room." Sure thing, he had company; I ran them off.

He had a rough side, but he also had a caring side. From a young boy, Shannon brought home teens needing help. Two in particular come to mind. One, a 15-year-old girl whose parents put her out. He brought her to our home and asked if she could stay. Of course,

I couldn't allow that. He told me later that he slept in the park on a bench to stay with that friend sometimes. It broke my heart that he was willing to give up his comfort for another. (The investigators did find the 15-year-old and returned her to her parents.) Another was a young man he shared his bedroom floor with, who is still in our lives today and checks on our family.

As an adult, Shannon thanked me often for teaching him how to read. He said because of it he could accomplish any job he gets without complications. His work ethic was phenomenal. He was remarkable when it came to seeking and keeping a job. He was always raised to management positions. This of course was not his testimony as a young, hot-headed teenager who would tell the employer what he thought, then leave and find another job.

Shannon was also good at saving money. I remember one day we were shopping when he was just a small tot. He looked up at me with those big brown eyes, pulling on my skirt, saying, "Mommy, you are a shopaholic." He just knew I was giving money away instead of holding onto it.

Shannon's Big Heart

From a rough teenager to adult stage, Shannon's morals and standards changed drastically. He was respectful, obedient, and everyone loved him – women, men, children, and employers. He had a winning attitude about himself and life.

Shannon would say, "Mom, the reason people mistreat me is because of this big heart you gave me. I hate it sometimes. When people see you are nice, they try to use you."

My reply was, "Son, never let anyone take that big heart away from you."

I always believed if anyone had a problem with Shannon, they needed to stop and look in the mirror because he wanted nothing but love for everyone. He had so many followers and touched many lives. He drew people, young and old. He had an aura about him that said, "You are accepted and loved!"

Shannon got joy out of mentoring young people. After his passing, the phone calls started pouring in, particularly the young men that he spent time instructing them about handling life's problems. We set up a mentoring program in his honor. The goal of Shannon's House was to impact teens' lives, their families, and eventually the community. This program consisted of counseling and support in areas of rejection, depression, suicide, and relationships. We connected with professional retirees from different backgrounds, such as police officers, school teachers, ministers, and coaches. They would volunteer their time when available. It was impactful. Sadly, we dropped the ball and it is no longer active.

My son's heart was as big as the sky. He helped everyone. Even if they mistreated him, he still held love in his heart for them. "I do not want hate in my heart to send me to hell," is what he would often say.

Shannon received salvation at an early age because I taught him about Jesus and the Bible. As a young boy, church was his foundation. I remember when I was a praise and worship leader. Shannon would sit on the first or second row and watch with such excitement as the Holy Spirit flowed through me as I ministered in songs. At age six, he was mesmerized by watching others and myself pray in tongues. One night in our family room, he told me he wanted to be filled with the Holy Spirit and pray in tongues. So I prayed with him to be filled and he went off to bed. As I was watching television with my husband, suddenly, Shannon, after being asleep for a while, walked in the room, laid on the carpet in front of us, and began speaking in tongues.

He always had a deep love for Jesus and the things of God. He would say to me from time to time, "Mom, I ask a lot of questions because I don't want to go off track." He was not ashamed of the Gospel of Jesus Christ and shared his faith when an opportunity presented itself. He ministered to everyone that was in need. Whether it was food, money, clothes, giving rides, etc., that was who he was. He was a giver and not a taker.

Shannon was the youngest of my three children, but you would think he was the oldest because he always made sure the family was strong and helping one another. After my husband passed, Shannon stepped into his father's role. He even told me that no one was going to walk me down the wedding aisle if I decided to do it again, except him.

"The only true friend I have," he would say. "Prayer Partner, Confidant, Support, and Pastor." That's who I was to him!

He would call me late at night and start off with his favorite words, "Hello, beautiful. What are you doing?"

My reply was always, "In the Word; the Bible."

He would then say, "You keep a book going now."

There were so many dreams in life he planned to accomplish, but never did. One of his dreams was for the family to start a restaurant business. (I am hoping this still comes to pass.) He was not just a dreamer; he was a planner and producer. His brother, Dwayne wrote his first rap song for him at age nine. This ignited Shannon's passion for writing songs and rapping at an early age. He produced some of his work before passing. His headstone is engraved with the label, "*ROA Realest Ofem All*,[9] Nonnahs."[10] (His son, Shannon Jr.'s rap name is Nonnash Jr.)

Oh how he loved his children. He became a father for the first time at age 19, so he knew he had to live for more than himself. He knew change must be permanent. He needed to plant his feet and become a provider, and that he did! He turned his life

---

[9] Shannon's production company's name
[10] Nonnahs is Shannon's name spelled backwards; his rap name.

around, 360 degrees. A true transformation! He proved to be so responsible that the courts awarded him custody of his two older children when they were ages 8 and 10 (Shannon Jr., 19 and Shanasia, 21 now live with me).

He loved them to the moon and back, but he kept them in check, including his two youngest (Shandon, 18 and Shalasia, 9). He had no patience for a disrespectful child. His character would not let him ignore issues that were out of order.

Shannon poured into his family principles to live by in order to be successful in life. He had Saturday morning sessions with them, imparting life skills, wisdom, and preparing them for the real world. Over the years, I watched so much being taken from him. He never had anything to show for being the hard worker he was and a provider for his family. At times, he was the mother and father, preparing meals after working over ten hours a day.

Satan launched an all-out attack on his family. In marriage, if the couple is not united, they will go under. Satan's number one weapon is to bring division in the home. He knows that a home divided against itself cannot stand (**Mark 3:25**). Shannon's children were the anchor that kept him in the married home despite it growing more toxic over the years.

After his marriage fell apart with his wife of 12 years, who is the mother of his two youngest, he met a young lady. They both cared for one another and started a life together. He began to show her the ways of God (doing devotionals and reading the Bible). They also started business ventures together (which are still growing with his name attached).

Some might say he should have waited until his divorce was cleared. My son, being a young, handsome man, wanted a relationship. He did not want to live alone because he was family oriented. People make their own decisions, so that is neither here nor there. As his mother and pastor, I gave him the right road to take. It was up to him to make the call.

Remember, anything you say or do contrary to God's Word is sin. As much as it hurts me to say this truth, I must say it for the sake of others who might be in the situation my son was in. Having a new companion without a legal divorce is sin. I do not condone wrong on any level. There is no way to dress up wrong. There is no right way to be wrong.

Satan is against marriages. If he can get either spouse to step outside of the marriage, that will give him access to come against them, which is an open door for his attack. God's desire is for us to stand, but once we reach our limit, what do we do?

My son was not religious, but he had a relationship with God. God knew his heart's desire. Shannon wanted to do what was right, so he eventually consulted a divorce attorney, but never got the opportunity to carry it out because his life was cut short.

His last words to me the night before his death were, "Mom, I do not like living this way. I want to do what is right."

Why So Soon?

So much life to live, so much love to give. In life we cannot always address every issue we face because some may be deadly. Shannon was the type of person that if something was out of order, he was going to address it. He would run to the roar. He even confronted gangs with guns before. He feared nothing.

Satan was always after his life. During my pregnancy, there were so many issues that could have been fatal, but God allowed Shannon to be born without harm. God called and anointed him to walk in the office of a healing evangelist. Shannon would say, "One day, Mommy, when I do not have to work so hard, I will walk in the call, but for now, I need to care for the family."

He was such a hard worker, working seven day a week sometimes. He always ministered to people while doing his daily chores at work. During his working hours, I would call him when I thought it was his lunch break and at other times when he was heavy on my heart. He would say, "You are feeling me, Mommy." I would let him vent and then we would pray. After working long hour days, on his way home, he would say, "Mommy, before going into my house, I always pray because I do not want to take spiritual forces from my workday into my house."

He was a peacemaker at heart. A few nights prior to his death, Shannon and his companion's 18-year-old son were having fun on FaceTime laughing as if all was well. My son spent a lot of time with him and was nothing but respectful to him, instructing him about life.

Shannon was not in a gang or in a night club, but in his home preparing breakfast when he decided to stop and address an issue, trying to bring peace between her and her son. The son shot Shannon in the torso four times with a stolen gun. I don't know the motive, but I have an assumption. I don't want to speculate something that I cannot prove, so I will have to wait because all the evidence is not in and the case has not gone to trial.

I tell myself sometimes, "If he had chosen not to address that issue, he would still be here with us." I do realize it does no good for me to play that over and over in my mind. *Woulda, shoulda, coulda.* Those three words cannot change any situation.

While we are walking this natural journey, there is a spiritual side we need not to ignore. Ignorance can and will bring premature death. **Ephesians 4:27** tells us to "neither give place to the devil" (KJV). There are many avenues where we give Satan access to our lives. Those who know to do and do not do, sin will open the door for Satan to attack your body.

My son contracted COVID-19 the last 10 days of his life. As he was in quarantine, we talked every night during his shut in. He was so proud to finally getting around to reading my first book, *Wounded but Healed*, but he did not finish it.

He spoke with me on Wednesday, February 24, 2021, as he rushed to the doctor's office to get his results thinking it was Thursday. We laughed about it. I told him, "Tomorrow, son." But tomorrow never came. Thursday morning, before going to his doctor, is when the altercation took place that led to my son's death.

I tell you nothing takes a child of God by surprise when you are in tune with His leading. Two nights before Shannon transitioned, God gave me a night revelation of his passing. He took one of our favorite moments (we had a lot of them) of us walking to school to pick up Dawn. He was a little boy again, maybe three or four years old. We walked into the school building, pushed the doors open, and began walking down a long corridor. Suddenly, Shannon began to cry those big tears. "Why are you crying?" I asked.

God also gave me another dream on that same night of Shannon and me going to the principal's office. Because I love the element of surprise, I wanted to scare him into thinking we were going because he was going to get in trouble. Again I asked him, "Why are you crying?"

He replied, "I don't want to be separated from my family."

I was touched by his response because his concern was for us and not what was about to happen to him from the principal. He thought if he got in trouble that would separate him from us. We reached the principal's office. The door was closed, the lights were out, and the office was dark. We took a seat outside and waited for the principal. As I began to sit Shannon on my lap, I woke up.

On Wednesday night, Shannon and I discussed the vision, but not the interpretation because he transitioned the next morning. I told him God showed me his heart. He got so excited, his voice was elevated on the phone.

"That's it, Mommy. I want God to see my heart," he said.

"He showed me your heart," I told him.

"That's what I want. I want him to know how much I love Him."

"He knows, son."

Before his passing, the week prior actually, he said to me, "Mommy, I just want some of God's peace."

My reply was, "Take His work, apply it, and you will have peace."

Sadly, he had to experience death to experience the peace God had for him on this earth. My son left his earthly family for a while, but is united with our heavenly family forever.

Am I in Denial?

Just because a person is not falling apart, crying every day, depressed, have no appetite, etc., does not mean they are in denial that their loved one has passed. There is no truth to that lie from Satan. Besides, all of the above will only make you sick. No one can tell you how to grieve because everyone grieves and process things differently. What works for one may not work for another.

Does denial exist? Absolutely. Denial happens when the mind refuses to accept the fact that they are gone and no longer here. The absence of their presence is proof enough. For grieving to begin, denial cannot coexist with reality; otherwise, healing could be prolonged. Avoiding and denying the loss will only bring more damage to the trauma.

I didn't fall completely apart because I still needed to function properly in my daily duties as a pastor, mother, grandmother, etc. Most importantly, God is my strength and the lifter of my head. Sometimes you don't know how strong you are in the Lord until something gut-wrenching, unexpected, and life-changing hits you.

It is times like these when we separate the warriors from the enlisted soldiers. I am on the war path. A quest. Shannon's death has caused the rise of many mighty men of valor and virtuous women of war on the arising – to mount up. A part of me was taken when Shannon died. Therefore, I am committed to fight even harder for the children of God that I come in contact with. I want to see every man, woman, boy, and girl under Satan's thumb to be loosed in the name of Jesus Christ.

Faith takes back what the devil has stolen. If the enemy is found, he must return seven-fold (**Proverbs 6:31**). I thank God by faith for the coming of my seven-fold, my spiritual sons and daughters, already established in the spirit realm with my mark on them. This is not replacing Shannon, because no one can ever do that. They are simply my harvest for the seed sown, his life.

Was I ever in denial? No, because I knew it was a reality, but I was in rage for a long time. Not with a person, but with death itself. Death is the last enemy to be destroyed (**Revelation 20:14**).

We don't know how much time we have on this earth, but God does. The secret things belong to Him. As stated in **Hebrews 9:27**, "It is appointed unto men once to die, but after this the judgment" (KJV). So we need to be strategic in how we live. We live and die by the choices we make (spiritually and naturally), so let us make Godly choices so we can lead productive lives, no matter how long we have.

Shattered, Not Broken

The morning of February 25, 2021, at 9:00 a.m., I was lying in bed as I received a phone call that resonated deep in my soul. On the other end was Jane (not her real name). She was screaming and crying that Shannon had been shot by her son. No details were given then, just that he had been shot multiple times.

As I was hearing the dialogue on the other end, I was wondering just how bad it really was. She asked the detective, "How bad is it?"

His reply was, "He was shot in the stomach and shoulder."

She asked the paramedics, "Do you have a pulse?"

They said, "Yes."

As they were putting Shannon in the ambulance, Jane said, "It did not look good."

My daughter, Dawn was in the other room. I gave her the news. We both got dressed and drove to the hospital. We could not go into the ER because of COVID-19 regulations. I gave the security staff my name as we waited to hear the status of my son's condition. I assumed he must have been surgery.

Forty-five minutes later as everyone gathered in the hospital's parking lot waiting for news from the staff, I sat in my car watching this scene from what seems like a movie. The news had come that my son, Shannon died from multiple gunshot wounds. We found out that he died in the ambulance on the way to the hospital. Family members began to pass out, falling to the ground. Others ran through the parking lot screaming and shouting, "They are lying!"

My response was neutral. *This cannot be happening. Not my baby. No, he is coming out of that hospital.* I could not cry. I was just numb. Somehow this did not take me by surprise.

That Tuesday, the Lord allowed me to present Shannon back to Himself as a little boy. As I stated earlier, Wednesday, Shannon and I discussed the dream, and now Thursday he is gone. God prepared my heart for this trauma.

"From the end of the earth I will cry unto thee, when my heart is overwhelmed, lead me to the rock that is higher than I" (**Psalm 61:2**, KJV). That scripture sums up how deeply losing my son affected my entire being.

We left the hospital and I called a family gathering at my house for prayer and questions. My house became a revolving door of phone calls and visits, nonstop. People poured in with condolences, food, drinks, and monetary gifts.

My heart was broken, shattered, scattered all over the place, fractured, destroyed, and impossible of being put back together. Or so I thought. I absolutely felt damaged, weak, and insubstantial, but God did not allow one piece to fall to the ground. **Psalm 34:18a** tell us, "The Lord is close to the brokenhearted and saves those who are crushed in spirit" (NIV). He kept me strong, not just for me, but for everyone else. I had to be a source of strength for the family. He assured me that I was going to be okay.

People have died from a broken heart. Knowing Jesus is the key to standing. Because the Father and I have an intimate relationship, He kept me afloat. He heard my cry, my plea, and immediately started the healing.

Know that crying does not mean you are weak; it's really a sign of strength. God gave us tear ducts for a reason. It is okay to cry unto God when your heart is overwhelmed. He is the Rock that is going to sustain you. The Rock that is higher than you. So don't hold back the tears. He sees our tears, collects them, and puts them in a bottle (**Psalm 56:8**).

If you cry while talking about your loved one, don't be ashamed of allowing the pain to flow from your heart. Your hurt and pain are real. God said when you are weak, then you are strong (**2 Corinthians 12:10**), because He takes over and strengthens you for the journey.

If I can compare my shattered heart to anything, it would be like taking an ax to a piece of thin glass; nothing is left but dust. God knows where every piece goes to be repaired and promises to do it for those who trust Him. Just like He caught every piece and began to mend them back together for me, He can do the same for you. Do you trust Him to do just that in your life as well? Do you trust Him to be who He says He is?

Insensitivity of the Heart

Peanut was sitting on the railroad track. His heart was full of butter. He didn't hear the 6:15, toot, toot, peanut butter.

When your 6:15 hits you, what is in you will come out of you.

We all have heard that the real person comes out at funerals and weddings. I can tell you I experienced a lot of that during this process. There were things that left me questioning if insensitivity and cold-heartedness were the norm in our society. I saw people for who they really are. The Bible tells us, "For out of the abundance of the heart the mouth speaks" (**Matthew 12:34b**, ESV).

Astonishingly, some people actually expressed joy over the loss of my son, making statements like, "He got what he deserved." You would think it came directly from Satan himself, which it did, because he uses people for his harmful purposes. I even had to block contacts and asked my family not to share any Facebook postings with me. But I tell you this, NO ONE deserves to have their life taken from them, no matter what caused it.

I'm sharing these things because healing is a process. I'm not trying to bash anyone, but simply providing an honest testimony, I believe, will help someone else overcome any problems they may be having in these difficult times.

Funeral planning in and of itself can be hard, especially if the couple is estranged and there's a lack of relationship or communication between the families, which was in my case. Shannon and his wife were separated and we had a difference of opinion regarding the funeral home his body would be released to. She made it very clear that because she was the legal wife, she was the only one who could turn the body over. I fully understood that at first.

Shannon passed on a Thursday, and after there was no contact or news on his whereabouts for a few days, I finally texted her a long message letting her know I needed to hear from her. She then contacted me letting me know where his body was located. Because it was the weekend (Saturday, in fact), I had to wait until Monday to speak with the coroner.

I had a few suggestions and asked her if she'd be willing to meet me at the funeral home to discuss arrangements. Her reply was, "I do not want to be in a room full of people who do not like me." So I went on my own and spoke with the funeral director, got all the information, but I did not choose them. I invited her along as well when I was interested in visiting another funeral home. Again, she replied, "No." So I went with my daughter and we made the arrangements, but we needed her to meet to finalize them. She then agreed to meet on the condition that I would not bring any family from my side; I kept my word.

We started moving forward with the funeral preparations, but not without discomfort from her family. One incident that stood out was the funeral home visit when she brought her family members to help finalize the arrangements. It was the three of them and me. She told me her reason for not contacting me was because she was trying to clear her head and she was being advised by family and friends to cremate his body and have a private ceremony. *Wow, so that was the reason for her initial silence?* I admit that was really painful to hear, and I felt it was cold and insensitive for someone to suggest such a thing. As we went forward, I saw how many had no concern for my feelings. I felt I was being punished because of the decisions my son made about his marriage. I just wanted him to have a proper burial.

The funeral director asked if we had any information regarding the state's advocacy program to help assist victims of crimes. One of her family members began repeating what the news reporters had reported about

my son's death with an angry voice tone.
When it was time to sign the legal
documents, that same family member asked
what she was signing because if victim
advocates do not pay... At that moment,
they began to fan their hand in my direction,
saying, "She, his mother, is paying, because
we are not paying anything."

My reply was, "We got this. If I need to
write a check, I will." And I did.

The estranged wife said she did not want a
family car. I said we did. Since she wasn't
paying a dime, like her family member said, I
requested to add one to the bill. She said she
was not going to ride in it.

We then went over the obituary. It was only
right to give her and her family the
opportunity to be on the program, but no
one cared to participate. One family member
told her that she would be a d@#! fool if she
attended the service. I think the family was
more concerned about her embarrassment
than the actual loss of my son. Given the

circumstances, I can understand why it would be embarrassing. I won't negate that at all. But, in the end, thankfully, victim's advocate program reimbursed the entire amount in full.

What I have shared was only a drop in the bucket compared to all the things I went through since my son's death. I cannot go into everything I suffered because of peoples' hard hearts. Finally, after going through all the drama, the day came (Friday, March 6, 2021) when it was time to lay my son to rest. I received the strength and honor from the Holy Spirit to eulogize him. His four children got up and spoke about their father as well. They were strong and powerful in expressing their love for him, and they vowed to carry on his legacy. This was a powerful move of the Spirit. But the most disrespectful thing I had to face was at the burial site when a fight almost broke out. The angry parties and their family became very loud, making it known they were upset.

This was total disrespect for my son who had not been laid to rest at that time.

Even though some detractors felt a certain way and tried to throw all of his accomplishments out of the window, they cannot take away from the fact that my son worked hard to care for his family while he was here. All the drama I experienced in planning his funeral was well worth it, because it made me a stronger person. Everything that has happened and is still happening has not changed me as a Christian because God is keeping me afloat. He is still fighting my battles.

I know I am not the only one who has and is even now as I'm writing this going through the same, if not the exact, situation. Walking that aisle to view the body of a loved one is never an easy thing. Whether it is during the death itself, the funeral planning, or the burial process, we can all suffer from insensitive people. But we should not alter our character because of the actions of others. When they trample on our heart, we must meditate on the truth and we will be strengthened. They may not ever ask us for forgiveness. Unforgiveness can become a stronghold in our lives if we let it. We have to break the chains of bondage. The antidote to this type of poison, even when it is hard, is the Love of God. So forgive them for you, not for them. (It is a process.) Like Jesus said on the Cross, "Father, forgive them; for they know not what they do" (**Luke 23:34a**, KJV).

Accepting the Loss

Only God can walk us through each day's pain, but we must first give it to Him. Once you give it to Him, do not feel guilty. Do not feel like you no longer love your loved one that has passed. That is another lie from Satan.

In the natural, your loved one's physical body is no longer here, but the memories you have of them are still alive and will always hold a place in your heart. If you are a born-again believer, you know that dying in Christ is never an annihilation or ceasing to exist, but rather a spiritual separation only for a season. Because of the natural separation, grief will take place and try to take a foothold in your life.

Grief is a mindset that will lead us down a destructive, depressing path, if we are not careful. We must take control over our emotions because we will go wherever our thoughts take us. "Change your thoughts –

change your life."[11] We can renew our mind through the Word of God.

During the first five months, I did not grieve my son because I had to deal with legal matters that I cannot speak about at this time. Writing this book has been therapy for me. My son's voice has ceased, but I am still alive to share his story from a mother's perspective.

Before Shannon passed, the Holy Spirit had me reading and studying materials on death. I kept saying to myself, "Someone is about to transition because God has me on this topic, so He must be preparing me for death." At the time, I didn't know whose death was imminent. In hindsight, knowing that He loved me enough to prepare me made it no less painful or easier to accept that loss, but it was easier to handle.

I eventually accepted the fact that Shannon transitioned, particularly knowing that there

---

[11] Wayne W. Dyer, 2009. Everyday Wisdom for Success

is a resurrection for those that sleep in Jesus (**1 Thessalonians 4:14**). However, knowing that he was never going to return to his home or family was the hardest part for me. Letting go of his personal possessions was difficult as well, but I did keep certain things to remember him by.

When I think about it, to ask the human frail mind to accept something so devastating, so painful, and so unfair seems impossible. With man it is impossible, but with God it is possible (**Mark 10:27**).

Some say they will never accept the loss of a friend or loved one because if they do that means they are letting go of them. To an extent that is true because you will eventually have to let go in order for God to mend your broken heart. We all have to give it to Him – our burdens, our pains, our tears – because we cannot handle them in our own strength. If we are to move on in life, we must accept this shift. Until we accept the loss, we will still be holding on, hoping that this is only a dream or nightmare that will eventually end.

Let me throw out this wind of caution. When you are grieving, you have to be careful because the devil will allow entities that look like, sound like, and have the same mannerisms as your loved ones to show up, trying to convince you that they are them. Out of desperation when one is having a hard time understanding, accepting, or grappling with the reality of the situation, one is more apt to believe they are. The person you think is your loved one is what the Bible refers to as a familiar spirit. You are then dealing with an evil spirit and not your loved one. One that is of the devil and not the Spirit of God.

Some may say, "Well, what's the big deal? My loved one's spirit is encouraging me." The Bible tell us that Satan has the ability to transform himself into an angel of light (**2 Corinthians 11:14**). Simply put, this is not of God. You must be careful not to receive advice from or have conversations with loss loved ones. They cannot help you or answer your why questions. **Ecclesiastes 9:5** says,

"For the living know that they shall die: but the dead know not any thing" (KJV).

You cannot deny the fact that your loved one is no longer here, but you can deny the enemy the right to get you over into a state of depression or confusion. If you begin communicating with the dead or trying to summon them up, you are entering into dangerous territories. That's called *necromancy*, or relying on "sprits of the dead for purposes of magically revealing the future or influencing the course of events."[12] You are moving over into divination, witchcraft, and sorcery, if you choose to do that. Satan's purpose is to get you to depend on the evil spirit and not the Holy Spirit. This familiar spirit will eventually lead you astray. So if you think you can hold on to your loved one through a familiar spirit, you are beginning to worsen your situation. To be absent from the body is to be present with the Lord (**2 Corinthians 5:8**), not present at your house.

---

[12] https://www.merriam-webster.com/dictionary/necromancy

I think because our mind does not want to let go of them it can put us in a vulnerable position. We cannot hold on so strong that our minds begin to play tricks on us. That's when you begin to see them and hear their voices. Satan will use that to your disadvantage, but to his advantage, just to torment you. It can happen to any one of us when we are vulnerable. Here is an example. One day my granddaughters and I went to one of Shannon's and my favorite restaurants. As I sat there, my eyes began to water thinking about all the times we shared. I thought I heard Shannon say, "No stressing, Mommy; no stressing. If anyone knows what is going on up here, you do. No stressing."

They are no longer here in the physical realm. The natural world has ended for them and they are not coming back. But the spirit realm, the real world, is just beginning. There is going to be a reunion in the heavens on judgement day, so accept the fact that it is not over for good, this is only the beginning of a new beginning to come.

The sooner you learn to accept your loss, the sooner your grief and the sting of death will lessen. The sooner you let go, the sooner your healing will begin. I promise you, each day the pain of your loss will become less painful. You may be saying, "This is easier said than done." Guess what? It is not easy, but it is doable.

I think sometimes how someone dies has an effect as well. For example, if their death was a sickness, we accept the fact that their body could no longer support itself and tell ourselves they had to leave for their new home, where they will have a glorified body. If it was from a tragic event, we accept the fact that justice will be served.

Overcoming grief has everything to do with your thought life. Are you mastering your thoughts or allowing them to run free? When tormenting spirits begin to rule your mind, you need to stop them in the very beginning. If not, they will begin a snowball effect, one thought after another causing strongholds. This will make it difficult to move on. **2 Corinthians 10:5** talks to us about, "Casting down imaginations, and every high thing that exalts itself against the knowledge of God, and bringing into captivity every thought to the obedience of Christ" (KJV).

You are the only one who can bring your thoughts into obedience. Your imagination is the incubator where things are conceived, therefore it is important to protect your eye-gate, ear-gate, and mouth-gate. Whatever you take hold of in abundance, you are meditating on it. If you hold the thought long enough, you will conceive it and eventually give birth to it. It is scientifically proven that if you hold a thought for 17 seconds, another one just like it will appear and then there is an explosion, which creates a stronghold. We have the power to build or destroy. If you do not want an unproductive thought to come to pass, then let go of it, abort it by casting it down, which removes it from your incubator; your place of conception.

If you need to rid yourself from bad thoughts or images, you can do it. You have the power to let it go. This means you have a part to play, and you must choose to let go of every negative thought and memory. **Let Go** so you can live, and **Let God** so you can be healed.

If that means watching the livestream of your loved one's funeral over and over, or visiting the grave site helps you, do what works for you. Know that there will come a time that you will need to get a balance and these things may no longer be productive for your life. If your life is consumed with your loss, then you have stopped living and do not even realize it. Dying is just as much a part of life as living is. I am not being insensitive, but I am reminding you that your loved one passed, not you. Life has not ended for you. Decide to pick up the pieces. I am admonishing you to get up and live.

Strong Support System

I am a person of prayer, but during the first days of Shannon's transitioning, I could not open my mouth to pray. I laid on my bed, moaning and groaning, not uttering a single word. Yet I am thankful because **Romans 8:26b** tells us, "but the Spirit itself maketh intercession for us with groanings which cannot be uttered" (KJV). Nothing can compare to the Holy Spirit interpreting what your heart is saying even though your mouth speaketh not. If you feel like you cannot pray while grieving, just lay or sit in the presence of God and let Him minister to your spirit, soul, and body.

I thank God that others were praying on my behalf and that there is no distance in the spirit realm, therefore, prayers can affect you and reach you thousands of miles away and transcend through time. Prayers will hold you up in your darkest hour. Believe me, in the beginning, you will have many dark hours.

During my time of despair, prayers and condolences were felt and made a difference as they flooded in like living waters. God hears prayers and He touches the hearts of others to pray for us when we need it as well. Being covered in prayer during your time of sorrow is the best thing you can have during this difficult time.

Having people surround you with love, sensitivity, and understanding can impart strength. If you do not know the importance of a strong support system, take my word for it, you cannot and will not make it without one. It is a must to have one in the beginning and thereafter.

Now, it is possible to have well-meaning people around and they may not be coming from a positive viewpoint, which will add to any stress that you have. That's where discernment kicks in. If they are not lifting you up for the better and are encouraging you to believe that it is okay to not get up and move on, or maybe pushing you toward drugs, sex, and alcohol as methods to numb your pain, then these are not the people you need to be around.

Let's take **Job** in the Bible, for instance. His friends were not true friends because all they did for days was bring out his faults, tried to persuade him (by jumping to conclusions) that he was sick, hurting, and thereby causing his own suffering because he sinned against God (**4-23**).

A network of spiritual people gearing you toward the things of God, praying and speaking into your life; now, their support can strengthen you physically and mentally. Trauma can change our brain and we need to have people speaking peace, healing, and love into our lives. Also, do not be afraid to pick up the phone and share your grief, whether it is with family, friends, or a pastor. Do not sit in the dark and vanish away from society. Allow others to cry, laugh, and reflect with you. We all need someone to help us, to hold up our arms like Aaron and Hur did to Moses as they sat a rock under him (**Exodus 17:12**). I too had to learn that this was not the time to shut away from people.

I even revisited "Footprints in the Sand" and drew comparisons to what I was going through. I have always loved that poem. It is about a man who had a dream that he was walking on the beach with the Lord. Scenes of his life kept flashing before him. He noticed that it was at his most trying time that when he looked in the sand all he saw was one pair of footprints. He asked the Lord, "Why?" The Lord replied, "It was at that moment I was carrying you." [13]

God wants to carry us through our impossibilities. We cannot get through this on our own. It is impossible from the flesh standpoint to do so. I pray that God will send you the right support person or persons, no matter if it is one or six; the

---

[13] Mary Stevenson, 1936

number does not matter. **Ecclesiastes 4:9-10** reminds us, "Two are better than one, because they have a good reward for their labour. For if they fall, the one will lift up his fellow: but woe to him that is alone when he falleth; for he hath not another to help him up."

You may have a lot of low moments, but refuse to stay there. Adopting a lifestyle of prayer, praise, and worship will bring you from depression to a level of joy. **Nehemiah 8:10b** tells us to "neither be ye sorry; for the joy of the Lord is your strength" (KJV). When we accept His provision of righteousness, by grace that reunites us so we can enjoy being in His presence.

In the supernatural realm, the strongest support system you can have is God, Jesus, and the Holy Spirit. They have promised to be our comforter, strengthener, helper, and standbyer. We cannot properly go through each grieving stage without their help. God does not expect us to carry any burdens. He cares for us and assures us that when we cast them to Him, He will sustain us (**Psalm 55:22**, KJV). Like a fisherman throwing his rod, cast it. Do not carry it. God wants you to throw the grief on Him. Let Him walk you through every stage. You cannot win the war without the Rock. He is bigger than your loss and greater than your gain. He is the only strong support that will not leave or forsake us (**Hebrews 13:5c**, **1 Kings 8:57**, **Psalm 27:9**). Whatever we need, the **I AM** God is present.

A Prayer for You

Father, in the name of Jesus, I come before you as intercessor for those who are grieving in any way, shape, or form.

You are our High Priest who knows what it feels like to suffer grief. You said in your Word that you have "borne our griefs and carried our sorrows."[14] Because you took our sins in your body to the Cross, it is by your stripes that we are healed.[15]

I pray today that you would give them strength to carry on because your plan for their lives still exists. It did not stop because of this loss.

I stand in the gap and pray for those who are surviving child loss or any type of loss. You see their tears and you hear their prayers. I pray that you, the God of all comfort, would comfort them through these words, and this

---

[14] Isaiah 53:4a, RSV
[15] 1 Peter 2:24

book would be an instrument to help them through their grieving stage.

I know you as comforter because my son is with you. Each day you comfort me through your love and your Word. Do the same for them, Father. I pray that they will see you in a light like never before and will come to want to serve you the rest of their lives. I pray that your light would shine upon them. Your light is your glory, and your glory is your presence. Let your presence be so evident to them that they will love being in it. In your presence, Father, is where the fullness of joy is.[16]

Thank you, Lord, that every day they are being strengthened and the sting of death is being lifted, they can lift their eyes unto the hills, from where their help comes from. Our help comes from you, Lord,[17] the maker of heaven and earth. You are our source!

AMEN.

---

[16] Psalm 16:11
[17] Psalm 121:1

Epilogue

What more can I say that I have not said already? I do not have favorites with my children. Everyone called Shannon my *Golden Child*. I believe because of the love we shared outweighed any obstacle we had to cross.

Shannon gave me many reasons to live. We had so much work to do together, but it was cut short. The rewarding part is knowing he was ready. I do not have to wonder if my baby made it into heaven. I know because of his confession of Jesus Christ as his Lord and Savior.

Tribute

June 27, 1979 – February 25, 2021

My Shannon, "Possessor of Wisdom," you are gone, but not forgotten. Every tear I drop for you, God catches it in His hand. I am living on this side carrying out your legacy. In my heart the words, **"REUNION, REUNION, REUNION"** are resonating. But not for now, my son, because I have lots of work to do for the kingdom. Just knowing this is not the end gives me joy. I'll see you on the other side in glory. Until we meet again, I love you, my son!

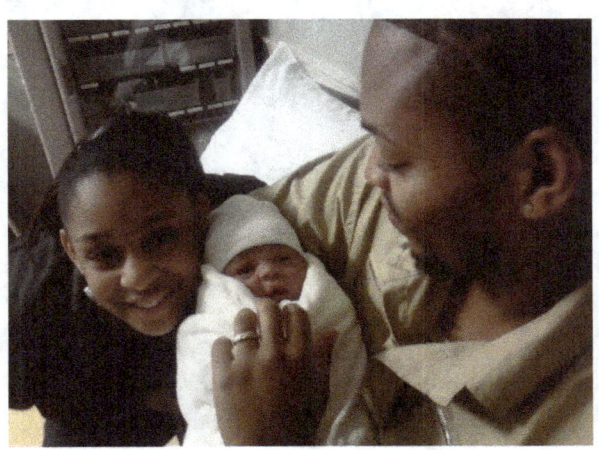

About the Author

LaVinia Young is the pastor and founder of Oasis

of Hope Outreach Ministry of E.C.C.M. in Columbia, South Carolina. She has a ministry heart for the needs of people. When she is not pastoring the flock, her passion is outreach, serving the community by evangelizing in prisons, jails, and wherever her Lord leads.

Lavenia loves cooking, journaling, and spending time in the presence of the Lord. She is the author of *Wounded but Healed*. She has traveled internationally to conduct divine healing meetings in Costa Rica.

She is a graduate of Charis Bible College with a degree in Biblical Studies. She's blessed with three young adult children, Dwayne, Dawn, and Shannon (who has transitioned to be with his Lord and Savior), and seven grandchildren.

www.ingramcontent.com/pod-product-compliance
Lightning Source LLC
Chambersburg PA
CBHW072016290426
44109CB00018B/2258